Seaport

Other poetry collections by Robert Hampson:

Assembled Fugitives: Selected Poems, 1973–1998
Seaport: Interim Edition
Feast of Friends
A City at War
A necessary displacement

Selected other publications:

The Salt Companion to Allen Fisher (with Cris Cheek)
New British Poetries: The Scope of the Possible (with Peter Barry)

Seaport

ROBERT HAMPSON

Shearsman Books
Exeter

This edition published in the United Kingdom in 2008 by
Shearsman Books Ltd
58 Velwell Road
Exeter EX4 4LD

www.shearsman.com

ISBN 978-1-84861-029-3

Acknowledgements
I am grateful to Michael Carlson for publishing part of section 4 as a
pamphlet, *A City at War* (London: Northern Lights, 1984); to Martin
Dodsworth for publishing 'growth-rings' in *English*; to Gilbert Adair
& Patricia Farrell for inviting me to read *Seaport* at Subvoicive; and to
Gilbert Adair for encouraging me to allow the complete incomplete text
to see the light of day.

An earlier version of Hilda Bronstein's essay appeared as a review
of *Seaport* in *Angel Exhaust* 15 (Autumn 1997). We are grateful to Hilda
Bronstein and the editor, Andrew Duncan, for permission to reprint the
essay here.

An earlier version of *Seaport* was published in 1995 by Pushtika Press,
London.

Contents

FOREWORD

When Robert Hampson first published *Seaport*, back in 1995, under the imprint of his own Pushtika Press, it was described as an 'interim edition', implying that a more complete and definitive one would follow in due course. It is especially pleasing, therefore, to be able to welcome this handsome new edition of a sequence which attracted an unusual amount of notice and comment for a small-press booklet when it first appeared.

Seaport deals with many aspects of the history and development of Liverpool, drawing on a wide range of documentary sources, and culminating with a vivid account of what the national press called the 'Toxteth Riots' of 1981. This event is seen in the context of the repressive policing methods of the day, especially as directed at black youths—one of the most unforgettable passages in the poem concerns 'a black 17 year-old/ arrested/ for dropping a chip-paper in Granby St', and then 'arrested again/ for "disturbing the peace"/ playing football'. All this is seen in the historical context of Liverpool's notorious role in the slave trade, and of subsequent patterns of racial discrimination, and the section is headed with an epigraph from Martin Luther King; 'A riot is at bottom the language of the unheard'.

The situation in the city has much improved since 1995, one symptom of that improvement being the International Slavery Museum, opened at the Albert Dock in 2007 (the bicentenary of abolition). It is an inspiring and hopeful place which celebrates resilience and inventiveness rather than defeat and victimhood. Long repressed aspects of the city's history have been aired since 1995, and it is now widely known, for instance, that Penny Lane is not the innocent-sounding childhood dream-place of the Beatles song, but is named after the 18th century Liverpool slave trader James Penny, a man who spoke in favour of the trade before a parliamentary committee in 1792 and was afterwards presented with a huge silver centrepiece for his dining table by grateful fellow-traders in the city. Liverpool had petitioned Parliament in 1788 asking it not to abolish the trade, and several of the signatories of that petition also have familiar Liverpool names, familiar because they are now the names of streets and buildings known to everyone who grew up in the city.

In many ways, the 1980s and its aftermath was Liverpool's bleakest post-war period: as well as 'Toxteth' in 1981, there was Heysel in 1985, Hillsborough in 1989, and the James Bulger murder in 1993, and the backdrop to it all was, as Robert says in the poem, that the city was 'the Carthage/ of Britain's de-industrialisation'. Thankfully, things seem much better now than then, with construction cranes everywhere, a massive student population, and thriving sports and entertainments industries. But the depth and permanence of these changes cannot be taken for granted, and this book, originally written in the late 1970s and early 80s, remains an important and highly informative work which uses poetry in a powerful documentary mode to draw attention once again to the abiding contradictions and inequalities on which our society continues to be based.

With this new edition, *Seaport* takes its place in a major tradition of post-war urban poetry in Britain, a tradition which operates in the big-scale, open field manner pioneered by Pound, Williams, and Olson, and re-invented and developed from the 1960s onwards by British writers such as Roy Fisher, Ken Smith, Edwin Morgan, Iain Sinclair, and Allen Fisher. Roy Fisher summed up the aim and essence of the method in his well-known pronouncement 'Birmingham's what I think with', and in *Seaport* Robert uses Liverpool for the same purpose, and with constant inventiveness. Indeed, the elements I first admired about the poem were the numerous variations and subtleties seen in the way it incorporates and finesses its many shards and fragments of 'extra-textuality', and I concentrated on that aspect of the sequence in my earlier discussion of *Seaport*. Today I value it no less for those qualities, but I also see it as a unique poetic investigation of the fabric and provenance of today's urban Britain, and, more particularly, as a powerful and moving portrayal of the native city which he and I have in common.

Peter Barry

Seaport

'A man does not know his own ADDRESS (in time) until he knows where his time and milieu stand in relation to other times and conditions.'

(Ezra Pound, *Guide to Kulchur*)

'The starting-point of critical elaboration is the consciousness of what one really is, and is "knowing thyself" as a product of the historical process to date, which has deposited in you an infinity of traces . . .'

(Antonio Gramsci, *Prison Notebooks*)

'He what was waving his rattle is now married
We what cheered Roger Hunt are getting on
And we don't bloody like it.'

(R. L Crawford, *The Scrap Heap*)

For Peter Barry, Nona Sheppard, John Simpson,
Jim Stewart, and Gilbert Adair.

plenty of nothing

back-to-back to
basics:
window, wall,
door—
damp yard-odour of
ashpits.

flat-capped
cropped
black moustache

stands by
yard-door to entry

broke his back
dockside
accident

a widow
5 children
2 more
died in infancy.

yellowing teeth
of the parlour piano

dust on the dresser

dull metal of marley horses
the lithe & muscular backs
of animals & men

Part I

LANDFALL AND DEPARTURE

'The term "Landfall" is more easily understood; you fall in with the land, and it is a matter of a quick eye and of a clear atmosphere. The Departure is not the ship's going away from her port any more than the Landfall can be looked upon as the synonym of arrival. But there is this difference in the Departure: that the term does not imply so much a sea event as a definite act entailing a process—the precise observation of certain landmarks by means of the compass card.

Your Landfall, be it a peculiarly shaped mountain, a rocky headland, or a stretch of sand-dunes, you meet at first with a single glance. Further recognition will follow in due course; but essentially a Landfall, good or bad, is made and done with at the first cry of "Land Ho!". The Departure is distinctly a ceremony of navigation.'

(Joseph Conrad, *The Mirror of the Sea*)

perch rock

ships   move in

            from the bay

close to the flat   coastline of crosby

                into the narrows

perch rock   stands

                to starboard

the close

        vestibular   landline

            runs

            from   the point blocks

                                of flats

to the graceful lines

            of dark-brick

                terraced houses.

seaport

'For centuries Chester had dominated the northwestern approaches when Liverpool was no more than a fishing village on the eastern bank of the little used river Mersey. As the Dee began to silt it was Neston which usurped Chester's position, port of embarkation for the English forces *en route* for Ireland. Liverpool, however, grew fat and prosperous on the takings of the slave trade and, buttressed by the swiftly expanding output of manufactured goods from the hinterland of Lancashire, the town witnessed rapid development.'

(Quentin Hughes, *Seaport*)

Between 1680 and 1760, the population of Liverpool grew from 4,000 to 40,000.

'This town has now become so great, so populous, and so rich, that it may be called the Bristol of this part of England.'

(Daniel Defoe, *A Tour through the Whole Island* . . .)

'The town has now an opulent, flourishing and increasing trade, not rivalling Bristol, in the trade to Virginia, and the English island colonies in America only, but is in a fair way to exceed and eclipse it, by increasing every way in wealth and shipping . . . Bristol lies open to the Irish Sea, so does Liverpoole: Bristol trades chiefly to the south and west parts of Ireland; from Dublin in the east, to Galloway west; Liverpoole has all the trade of the east shore and the north from the harbour of Dublin to London Derry. Bristol has the trade of South Wales; Liverpoole great part of the trade of North Wales; Bristol has the south west counties of England . . . though they may rival one another in their appearances, in their number of shipping, and in several particulars, yet they need not interfere with one another's business . . . One has all the north, and the other all the south of Britain to correspond in. As for Wales, tis, as it were, divided between them by nature itself.'

(Defoe, Ibid.)

the docks

winter on the mersey

the ships ride   in the open road

  or   haled ashore

   lie on their sides in the mud

then   1710

 by act of parliament the first wet-dock

    (the first private wet-dock out of London)

  right-angled to the river

   the high-masted ships

     penetrate the city

   masts mix with the city skyline

     the terraced houses & churches

'a town of so much trade'

 but already : the problems

   the bigger ships that enforce obsolescence

   the dangers of silting

1748 : the *Queen Elizabeth* takes 16 tides

     to be floated into the Mersey

  while the other traders queued

     lay exposed in the Narrows

docks (2)

deep penetration

        gives way to a lineal system

Hartley   pushes the docks

          north & south along the coast

     Brunswick Dock (1832)

     Clarence Dock

        etc.

a seven-mile line of docks

     cuts the city off from the river

     cuts masts & funnels out

       of the daily life of the town

and Hartley's massive dock-walls

   18ft curtain-walls & castle-towers

        splits the docks from the dock-road

    the docks   fortified against

        pilfering

  heavy wooden gates

    slide   with precision

  along iron guide rails   deep into the walls

      these stronghold images

the Victoria Tower   1848.

the docks: the emigrant trade

1.

in 1807

        the last year before Abolition

185 Liverpool ships

        carried 49,213 slaves

by 1850

        the city that once had

                five-sixths of the slave trade

                now had

                two-thirds of the British emigrant trade

        timber from the American north

        cotton from the southern states

        emigrants

                for the return trip

in 1847

        emigrants paid $5m. in fares

        subsidised freight on the N.Y. packets

'Today Liverpool is the grandest English city outside London.
The centre of no other English city is planned on such a scale.'

profit from slaves, cotton, & emigrants

St George's Hall

begun 1839

completed 1854

'a monument to money'

by 1847

the city had ten newspapers

ship launches

regattas

'public' dinners & assemblies

& the largest stock of cloaks & mantles in the country

in the finest fashions.

Hawthorn was given the consulship   1853–1857

as the best gift the US could offer.

2.

Hawthorn did not meet

> Thackeray, Dickens, Charles Reade, or
> George Eliot

he saw Tennyson

> across a picture-gallery

he said the Mersey

> had all the colour of a mud puddle
> and no atmospheric effect
> ever changed the tinge

every day

> he walked the city

> > 'the people are as numerous
> > as maggots in cheese'

the men were

> haggard, drunken, care-worn

Tithebarn Street

> was thronged with dreadful faces

                              an army of the poor

        old women

                dried up

                              with slow starvation

        young girls

                        incurably sick

'he never walked these streets
without feeling he might catch some disease'

        one man   held a painted board on his knees
                       showed himself caught
                       in the cogs of a machine.

3.

between 1846

and   1855

nearly three million people emigrated from Britain

the majority   from Ireland to North America
                                          by way of Liverpool.

the famine of 1846
          (more fully reported in Canada
                    than in the British press)
was followed by typhus in 1847
& for the first time
                    Poor Law
was applied to Ireland
                    the landlords
'shovelled out'
                    their tenants:
£2 per head   per year   for the workhouse
where £4   bought a permanent passage.

the biggest ships
          carried a thousand steerage passengers
          the deck-space   kept clear for the cabin passengers
          the emigrants   spent the 4 to 7 week journey

                                        under hatches

          'stowed away like bales of cotton'

          'packed like slaves in a slave-ship'

     treated *worse*   than slaves or cotton

     nobody lost   if the emigrants didn't arrive

     in 1848   the *Ocean Monarch*

     caught fire & sank   in the Mersey

     all the first-class passengers

                                        were saved

     a long list was published

                         of dead steerage emigrants.

the emigrants   were defrauded

               from the day they started their journey

                    up to(& after) they arrived in New York

it was   very big business

before they got to their ship

they'd had dealings with brokers

runners

lodging-house keepers

& keepers of stores

the emigrants were sold

bad food & unnecessary

pocket-mirrors, razors, bowie-knives

pistols & telescopes

27,000 people   lodged in 7,000 cellars

William Tapscott

had one brokers office in 1847

by 1855   had two offices & a private house

& an untaxed income of £8,400 p.a.

'Both Whig and Tory governments did as little as possible,
thinking it wrong to interfere unnecessarily with trade.'

PART II

SPUN-YARN

'At sea, the sailors are continually engaged in 'parcelling', 'serving', and in a thousand ways ornamenting & repairing the numberless shrouds & stays; mending sails, or turning one side of the deck into a rope-walk, where they manufacture a clumsy sort of twine, called spun-yarn . . . For material, they use odds & ends of old rigging called 'junk', the yarn of which are picked to pieces, and then twisted into new combinations, something as most books are manufactured.'

(Herman Melville, *Redburn*)

the chart

dedicatory letter to herman melville

and with slow elaborate phrase structure
is forged a migratory grammar
information to be loaded
distribution adapted to additional clues

the tacit assumption
that weight can equal space

that the set-up quantities & forces of language
make up syntactic structures
that balance the blanks

ships   hulls   tides   winds   currents

the storm   the action   the whales

held
in a single sentence
that by some specifying motion of its swell
suggests
precise expression

through the carefully-adjusted tensions

of ambiguities

the depths & latitudes of language

spunyarn

1.

June 3, 1839

> Herman Melville
> 'boy' on the packet-ship *St Lawrence*
> 3-masted, square-rigged
> > coppered & copper-fastened

> from the East River
> to the Mersey

> from Pier 14
> at the foot of Wall Street

> with the first of the flood
> > stood into the Mersey
> worked up to a berth
> > in Prince's dock.

2.

the sight of these mighty docks—
China Walls of masonry; a succession of
granite-rimmed docks,
completely enclosed, but linked
like the Great Lakes
or like a chain of immense fortresses:
Prince's Dock, George's Dock, Salt-House Dock,
Clarence Dock, Brunswick, Trafalgar . . .

nothing can exceed
the bustle & activity
of these quays:
bales, crates, boxes, cases
tumbled about by thousands of labourers;
trucks pass to & fro; dockmasters
shout; sailors of all nations sing out
at their ropes—the roar resounding
from the walls that hem all in.

the picture of Liverpool

The Picture of Liverpool

> *Stranger's Guide*
> *& Gentleman's Pocket Companion*
> (1803)

of Liverpool & the Mersey
    its docks & ships & warehouses
I sing:

> *Now o'er the wondering world her name resounds,*
> *From Northern climes to India's distant bounds—*
> *Where'er his shores the broad Atlantic laves*
> *Where'er the Baltic rolls his wintry waves.*

in Lancelot's Hay
    old women sort rubbish
    for pieces of cotton

    rake over dirt
    from holds of ships
    for pickings

at the dock-gates
    when the sailors leave
    run the gauntlet
    of a 'long lane of pauperism'

> 'Every variety of want & suffering . . . met the eye,
> and every vice showed here its victims.'

'the picture of all that is dishonourable
to civilisation & humanity'

lines of silent beggars
their pleas
chalked on the flags
records
in an hour's time
destined to be obliterated.

a committee of one

'Of all seaports in the world, Liverpool, perhaps, most abounds in all the variety of land-sharks, land-rats, & other vermin, which make the hapless mariner their prey. In the shape of landlords, bar-keepers, clothiers, crimps, and boarding-house loungers, the land-sharks devour him, limb by limb; while the land-rats and mice constantly nibble at his purse.'

(Melville, Redburn)

Item One: by the dock-wall:

> notices of departure
> advertisements for clothes
> handbills for doctors
> rat-trap ads
> for army & navy enlistment
>
> spirit-vaults
> pawnbrokers
> peddlers of razors
> merchants of brass-jewellery.

Item Two: downtown:

        tens of thousands
        of rags & tatters
        men, women, & children
        with evening
        empty themselves into the streets.

        endless vistas of poverty:
        want & woe arm-in-arm
        beggary before—
        & at my heels.

Item Three: Brunswick Dock:

> vast quantities of produce
> imported from starving Ireland:
> decks turned into pens
> for oxen & sheep;
> deck-passengers
> penned-in like cattle—
> Irish labourers
> to bring in
> the English harvest.

Item Four: Merchants' Exchange:

flagged quadrangle; colonnades;
brass statuary:

Nelson dying; a wreath hovers
over his sword-point; death
reaches for his heart.

round the base:
captives in chains,
emblems of Nelson's victories:
the limbs & manacles
of slaves
in the marketplace.

Item Five: the 'Old Church' of St Nicholas:

the 'dead house' in the basement:
bodies of the drowned
exhibited till claimed.
old men & women
watch the docks for bodies
for the standing reward.

no misery
that cannot be rendered
marketable.

PART IV

THE LEAVING OF LIVERPOOL

'I don't know about the history. The people who are in control & in power & the class system & the whole bullshit bourgeois scene is exactly the same except that there is a lot of middle-class kids with long hair walking around London in trendy clothes & Kenneth Tynan's making a fortune out of the word "fuck". But apart from that, nothing happened except that we all dressed up. The same bastards are in control, the same people are runnin' everything, it's exactly the same. They hyped the kids & the generation.'

(John Lennon, *Lennon Remembers*)

growth-rings

layer by layer

tools   weapons   shards of pots

bones

stone   bronze   iron

history   seen as   technological change

antler-hoes   ards

beam-engine   steam-train

transistor

born

when the records   changed speed

pre-history now

economic organisation / social change

uses

botany / archeology / atomic physics

whatever comes to hand

radio-carbon dating

checked by   bristlecone-pine growth-rings

rectified   re-

writes   history.

you can't dance to art

(merseybeat 1962–64)

a suburban
music shop
youth in a
collarless
jacket
fingers the
chord
A minor
on guitar
cuban-heeled
boot rests on
tiny amp
Vox AC30
(amp &
speaker
combined)
you could
carry it
yourself

the simplicity.

st thomas st: requiem & blues

1. another mirror: 1962–65   *(for guitars and harmonica)*

i.   irish
country & western

black music
brought back
from america

ii.   how hip
we were:
in Mathew St
in shades.

Howlin' Wolf
Little Richard

sweat
on cellar walls

brown ale
on the ferry.

iii.   *open up your eyes*
tell me
what you see

you can't cry
cos you're laughing at me

iv.   flash, brash
        obnoxious

        but
        total commitment

        to getting wrecked
        & getting laid.

2. mystery tour: 1965–68

'all starry it was & beautiful,
& them just sticking their fingers through it'

i.   *dank days & steamy nights*

the jacaranda
the casbah
the blue angel

lunch-time
& dance-hall sessions

hound dog
heartbreak hotel
blue suede shoes

luxemburg's
coded messages
blurred with static
punctuated with commercials.

ii.   *mystery tour*

a)   in a yellow-cab
       through the avenues
       of early dusk
       to a magic skyline

       a market
       ripe for exploitation

       then on
       through the night
       to another airport
       another sky
       the same madness

b)   cities shimmer
       already half-hallucination

       guitars buzz
       heavy feedback
       through the brain

       songs produced on buses
       & planes,
       in hotels & dressingrooms,
       in a space cleared
       among newspapers & teacups.

c)   (everybody had a hard year)

        records selling in millions
        bring in a farthing per disc

        concerts producing vast profits
        for cinema circuits, promoters,
        barely paid travelling expenses.

        ripped off by merchandisers,
        freeloaders, upmarket-seatwarmers.

3. out of frame: 1968–70

teargas.
threats of violence.
rubber bullets.

'you sell out,
bit by bit,
until
complete craziness
surrounds you.'

'war is over'

unreality's
the programme
of the day

'war is over'

unreality's
the programme
of the day.

a city at war

(Liverpool 8: 1976)

1.   poverty & bitterness.
the gap between 'them'
& 'us'.

fire-blackened windowframes.
broken bricks.   glass.

shopfront after shopfront
bricked or boarded.

corrugated iron.

'at the end of 2 hours
I realised
I'd not seen a tree,
a blade of grass,
a café, a dance-hall, a cornershop.'

2.   the long empty waterfront.

the falling-off
    of the cotton trade
in the 1930s

& the shift of sea trade
    from ocean routes
to mainland europe

completed
    the decline
        of the port.

3.   skilled labour
            drawn off to the peripheries
            to the new towns
        by 'job creation'
            since the 50s

        'city of change & challenge'

        the city centre
            eviscerated
        in 'urban redevelopment'

            flattened
        for motorways,
                carparks,
                        shopping-centres

        the Cavern knocked down
            makes space for an airshaft
        for the underground railway

            to bring commuters
                    in from the Wirral.

new brighton

'if ever a town died in sympathy for its city elder
. . . then it's new brighton'

'across the water'
the muddy
brown mersey
by ferry

20,000 visitors a week
in the 60s
now down to 500

you can hear
the tide
coming in

as the dole queues
grow
in Liverpool

& the throbbing of engines
from
the Seaforth Docks.

a better tomorrow

'trade has been the life-blood of Liverpool, and the port its heart'

1.   the flat-dwellers of Netherley, Kirby, Speke
       the shattered docklands
              of Toxteth, Scotland Road
       witnesses to the crisis
              of the 'mixed economy'

       1 in 6 of Merseyside's men & women
              without work
       50% unemployment round the North Docks
       40%   for the South Docks & Speke

       (the young, the black, & women
              bear the brunt)

2.	busts of blackamoors & elephants
in the town hall corridors:
reminders of the slave-trade.

returns never fell below 30%
at times: 100% (even 300%) profit.

monopolised by 10 large firms.

commerce, finance—
no industrial base.

3.   London, Detroit, Paris, Tokyo, Zürich:
          the centres of power.

       decisions determine the future
            of 3/4s of Merseyside's workers.

       plant expendability for higher profits:

            exodus of capital.

4. Dunlop
    Massey Fergusson
    Girling
    Meccano
    Standard
    Vauxhall

    all gone

    city of the dead.

July 1981

'A riot is at bottom the language of the unheard.'
(Martin Luther King)

1.   i.   1919: a white mob
roams Liverpool 8
for blacks

Charles Wooton
chased by the mob
drowns in the Mersey

the Charles Wooton Centre
(Upper Parliament St)
did *not* burn in 1981.

    ii.   National Westminster Bank
facing Upper Parliament St
sprayed **THE GHETTO**
as boundary-marker

burned: Sunday, July 5, 1981

the Rialto
owned by the Swainbank family
(former tory city councillor)
burned: July 5, 1981

the Raquets Club
(Upper Parliament St)
wood-panelling, uniformed barstaff
white sports-clothed families
where judges stayed over

burned: July 5, 1981.

iii.   *who owns Shell?*
       who owns Tesco's?
       who owns the banks?

2.   **policing the community (before)**

i.   3 young blacks
         in a car
         stopped by the police.

         all the windows
         smashed in
         with batons.

         'when asked by the defence
         if he could think of any reason
         why the car's <u>*rear*</u> *window*
         had been smashed in,
         a detective replied—
         "I think it was excitement
         on the part of the police".'

ii.   the driver
lost a front tooth
had 2 fingers
turned back to front
while transported
handcuffed
in a police van.
in court, no officer
could say
which policemen
were in the van
with the prisoner.
the police-driver had
no idea
what was going on
behind him.
one officer
testified to being
in the back of the van
but he was seated
so that he couldn't see
what was happening.

iii.   a black 17 year-old
         arrested
         for dropping a chip-paper
         in Granby St

         arrested again
         for 'disturbing the peace'
         playing football

         arrested again
         loitering
         with a group of friends
         at a bus-stop

         police-defined 'crime'.

3. policing the community (the riots)

i. *kenneth oxford orders cs gas to be used*

> high-velocity
> cs bullets
> barricade-penetrating
> cartridges
> capable of going thro walls
> *not* to be fired at people
> fired directly
> into crowds

> 5 people injured
> (all male,
> all black).

ii. *kenneth oxford decides to use police vehicles driven at speed to disperse rioters*

> one man's back
> broken

> david moore (22)
> a disabled man
> visiting his sister
> killed:

dragged along
by a police
'hit-&-run
driver'.

iii. *kenneth oxford wants armoured cars*

the leaving of Liverpool

empty warehouses
decay along the Mersey

21 dead acres of
the old Tate & Lyle plant

Liverpool: the Carthage
of Britain's de-industrialisation.

browned ink
& pencil scrawl

a palimpsest of
brick & tile
& stone

the partially-
effaced
traces
of previous statements.

the fabric
of these lives.

APPENDIX:

From Section III

A Picture of Roscoe

(after Washington Irving)

the elegant historian of the Medici
        among the busy sons of traffic
in the very marketplace of trade

not shut up in some garden of thought
but hours & seasons
snatched from the pursuit of worldly interests

the picture of active virtue
like his own Lorenzo
interweaves the history
of his life
into the history of his city

that union of commerce
& intellectual pursuits
diverts the tide of wealth
from the channels of traffic
to refresh the garden of literature

to awaken the ambition
of mental improvement
among the citizens.

Roscoe: To his books

'Every city of Italy a new Athens, and
Liverpool a new Florence.'

a spacious mansion of freestone
built in the Grecian style.

beyond the study windows
the Mersey winds
through an expanse of meadow,
Welsh mountains melt
into the distance

the library sold by auction:
black-letter bargains,
Roscoe's silent companions,
'loved associates, chiefs of elder art',
dispersed about the country.

Author's note to the interim edition, 1995

Seaport was written during the late 70s and early 80s, the latest parts being written during and after the riot of 1981. The unemployment statistics are taken from *Merseyside in Crisis* (Manchester Free Press, 1980), and don't reflect the impact on Liverpool of the economic miracle of the 1980s. *Seaport* has remained unpublished until now because Part III, 'The Rialto', has not been completed. In an interview in *Angel Exhaust* 8 (Autumn 1992), Gilbert Adair's reference to *Seaport* (as *Leaving of Liverpool*) has prompted this publication of an 'interim edition'. Fragmentary parts of Part III are included as an appendix.

Afterword: Spun Yarn

Seaport is a history of crises in the social development of Liverpool. Written over a period during the seventies and early eighties, it remained unpublished as Part III, 'The Rialto', had not been completed. Hampson was persuaded to publish an 'interim edition' in three parts (I, II, and IV with an appendix containing two fragments of the elusive part III) in 1995.[1] Michael Carlson had earlier published Part IV as *A City at War* in 1985.[2] This new edition includes an additional dedicatory poem, but the third section still remains incomplete.

Seaport is a poem of place; but unlike Roy Fisher's fictive 'City' or Allen Fisher's South London of 'unfelt forces', Liverpool's maritime location renders it a place of passage and transition, through which thousands of travellers, sailors, slaves, and immigrants have passed since the late 17th century. This seaport is now a palimpsest, which bears the contradictory traces of power and poverty, privilege and displacement. Inscribed into both texts, poem and city, are the signs not only of the wealth of those who had profited by the growth of the cotton industry and slave trades, but also of the struggle for survival of the inhabitants who lived and died there, and the cargoes of dispossessed human beings who had passed through.

> browned ink
> & pencil scrawl
>
> a palimpsest of
> brick & tile
> & stone
>
> the partially-
> effaced
> traces
> of previous statements

the fabric
of these lives.

The various transformations of Liverpool from fishing village to major seaport have resulted in the urban decline which stands in this volume as a symbol of capitalism and commodification, the embodiment of the social failure which is the consequence of commercial 'success'. For Hampson there has been 'no misery/ that cannot be rendered/ marketable'. By 1850, as well as profiting from the importation of timber from America and the export of cotton, 'the city that once had five-sixths of the slave-trade/ now had/ two thirds of the British emigrant trade'. This narrative is now inseparable from the topography of the city itself, its housing, docks, city centre, landmarks such as the Merchants' Exchange, where the statuary bears the 'emblems of Nelson's victories/ the limbs & manacles/ of slaves/ in the marketplace', and the 'Old Church' of St Nicholas where, in the basement, 'bodies of the drowned/ were exhibited until claimed'.

Hampson weaves a dense intertextual web which invokes the voices of those connected in some way with Liverpool and the sea, from Daniel Defoe and Herman Melville to John Lennon. For example, Joseph Conrad's definition of the term 'landfall' outlines the process whereby landmarks are recognised by sailors when approaching a destination. In the poem 'perch rock' the reader must navigate her way towards the string of signifiers by which this particular seaport is to be identified. The channel carved through the open field of the page replicates the narrow straits through which ships passed to enter the port.

perch rock stands
        to starboard

the close

```
        vestibular              landline
                runs

             from        the point blocks

                              of flats

    to the graceful lines
              of dark-brick
                    terraced houses.
```

The rape of the landscape, when in 1710 the first wet-dock allowed the 'high-masted ships' to 'penetrate the city' is similarly illustrated in the rupture of the linear form of the poem 'the docks', and later dockland developments described in 'docks (2)' mean that finally the essential connection of river and city is sundered as 'deep penetration/ gives way to a lineal system/ . . . / a seven-mile line of docks/ cuts the city off from the river'.

Part I is an amalgam of statistical and historical data, clippings from newspapers, advertisements, broadsheets and reports, and among them quotations from the diaries and letters of the novelist Nathaniel Hawthorne, US consul from 1853–57, for whom:

> 'the people are as numerous
>   as maggots in cheese'

The poet's voice is subsumed within the intertextual fabric, while the notion of seaport as constructed out of the lives and vicissitudes of those who lived and passed through her is fused with that of poem as a montage of words and phrases, documentary records and data, a scrapbook of the recorded moments in the histories of people and place. The words of Herman Melville are quoted, as he describes the sailors' method of picking to pieces 'odds and ends of old rigging called "junk"', and twisting them into new and usable twine known as 'spun yarn'. Melville draws a parallel between that procedure and the strategy by which 'most books are manufactured'.

Hampson weaves this metaphor into 'the chart', the opening poem of Part II, which he dedicates to Melville. In an exploration of 'the depths and latitudes of langauge', a correspondence is implied between the poetic process, the quest for 'precise expression/ through the carefully-adjusted tensions/ of ambiguities', and the hazardous voyage in pursuit of the whale. The open form and multiple significations of 'the chart', which juxtaposes the vocabularies of physics, linguistics, maritime tradition, and cartography, is in contrast to the tighter form and rhythm and the masculine language employed in the description of the docks themselves in the piece which follows it, 'spunyarn':

> China Walls of masonry; a succession of
> granite-rimmed rocks,
> completely enclosed, but linked
> like the great lakes
> or like a chain of immense fortresses

The final section of *Seaport*, Part IV, charts the period from the sixties to the early eighties, with allusions to Howlin' Wolf, Little Richard and the popular music which came out of Liverpool, and with the injunction to 'open up your eyes/ tell me/ what you see'. For a moment the poet's voice becomes subjective, 'how hip we were: in Mathew St/ in shades', as a narrative born of the poet's subjectivity forms another strand in the poetic weave. Hampson's pre-occupation with time, place and history is foregrounded in the first poem of this final group, 'growth rings', which brings together the notion of radio-carbon dating (a method of determining the date of organic material) with that of the writing (or righting?) of history. This final sequence speaks of police intimidation, riots, economic and social decay. In the ironically titled 'a better tomorrow' (taken from an earlier civic programme) are listed the statistics of expendability as unemployment, determined by decisions taken in distant power centres ('London, Detroit, Paris, Tokyo, Zürich') transform what had once been an active commercial centre and seaport into 'a city of the dead'.

'July 1981' is a fragmented account of the riots which took place in that month, interspersed with reports of the police brutality which typified them and the intimidation of young blacks which continued after the riots had ended. In the place which had prospered as a result of the slave trade, the topography is once again transformed as buildings which had served as the symbols of that wealth and power are destroyed by rioters:

> the Racquets Club
> (Upper Parliament St)
> wood-panelling, uniformed barstaff
> white sports-clothed families
> where judges stayed over

> burned: July 5, 1981

This multi-dimensional and multi-faceted text is an extraordinary concatenation of significations. It is a thought-provoking piece, not only because of its social dimension—or of its concerns with poetry as production. There is a constant interaction between the notions of time and space. The poem is situated in a chronologically documented social history (time) and in the mapping of the physical site (place) of Liverpool. The nexus between these two is an impulse towards a deconstruction and *re-reading* of historical texts. *Seaport* is concerned with the corruption and devastation wrought by capital, and the multiplicity of contradictory meanings contained in the discourses of recorded, and seemingly factual, history. It is a self-reflexive work, set in a textual field of histories, data, scientific knowledges and literature, and written in a language which speaks of the politics of desire and the eroticism of power which rapes the landscape in the name of capital and consumerism, dehumanizing millions as it does so. Moreover, the inclusion of the incomplete Part III, 'The Rialto', as an appendix (incidentally, the only section of the poem that strikes a note of optimism)) serves to emphasise the poet's concern with the notion of time as a continuing present, in which both past events and actions continue to take effect. Since the 'history' of Liverpool, and consequently both Liverpool the place and *Seaport* the text, are still in process, there can be no appropriate moment for closure to occur.

Hilda Bronstein

An earlier version of this appeared as a review of Seaport *in Angel Exhaust 15 (Autumn 1997). We are grateful to Hilda Bronstein and the editor, Andrew Duncan, for permission to reprint the essay here.*

Notes

[1] Robert Hampson, *Seaport: Interim Edition* (London: Pushtika Press, 1995).
[2] Robert Hampson, *A City at War* (London: Northern Lights, 1985.